Songs of praise

A book of 30 Bible readings and notes to
help you worship and pray

by Tony Phelps-Jones

Published by Scripture Union, 207–209 Queensway, Bletchley, MK2 2EB, England.

Email: info@scriptureunion.org.uk
Internet: www.scriptureunion.org.uk

© Copyright Causeway PROSPECTS
First published by Scripture Union in 2004, Reprinted 2010
ISBN 978 1 84427 066 8

Causeway PROSPECTS is a division of PROSPECTS for People with Learning Disabilities, and their address is PO Box 351, Reading, RG30 4XQ. Phone 0118 9516 978. Email: causeway@prospects.org.uk

About Causeway PROSPECTS: Causeway PROSPECTS provides resource materials and training to equip churches for effective outreach and ministry among people with learning disabilities. It also runs holiday weekends and special ministry at Spring Harvest and the Keswick Convention.

British Library Cataloguing-in-Publication Data: a catalogue record for this book is available from the British Library.

Scripture portions are taken from The Holy Bible: English Version for the Deaf (published as the Easy-to-Read Version) © 1995 by World Bible Translation Center, Inc. and used with permission. Internet: www.wbtc.com

Icons © Widgit Software Ltd 2002, developed by the Rebus Symbol Development Project, designed by Cate Detheridge, and used with kind permission.

Cover design by David Lund Design, Milton Keynes.

Printed by Marston Book Sevices Ltd.

⤷ Scripture Union: We are an international Christian charity working with churches in more than 130 countries providing resources to bring the good news about Jesus Christ to children, young people and families – and to encourage them to develop spiritually through the Bible and prayer. As well as our network of volunteers, staff and associates who run holidays, church-based events and school Christian groups, we produce a wide range of publications and support those who use our resources through training programmes.

How to use this book

 These daily notes are intended to help you to worship and to pray. Each day there is a short reading from the Bible, some thoughts and a prayer.

 The readings are from the *Easy-to-Read Version* (ETRV), a very clear and simple translation of the Bible. The reading printed each day is quite short. A longer reading is also given if you would like to read more using your own Bible.

The Bible, which is sometimes called the Word of God, is not really one book but a whole library of many books. The 66 books were written by many people that God spoke to at different times. At the front of the Bible you will find a list of the titles of all the books in the Bible and the page number where each book begins.

To help you find your way around such a big book, little groups of one or two sentences have been numbered, and then groups of those sentences have been collected into chapters.

So how do you find the one or two sentences that you want in the Bible? Let's say you want to find Matthew 5:5,6. That means you need to look in the book called Matthew, in chapter number 5 and verses 5 and 6.

You can find Matthew in the lists of books at the front of the Bible. In the *Easy-to-Read Bible*, Matthew starts on page 1109. So when you have turned to the beginning of Matthew you then search for chapter 5, which is on page 1113. Look down the page until you see the numbers 5 and 6. Those are the sentences (or verses) that you need.

When you do your Bible reading, try to spend a few extra minutes praying and worshipping.   Prayer is talking and listening to God. You can do this aloud or without using words.   You can pray on your own or with friends.   Worship is telling God how much you love him, through words or songs, or things you do.   This can be singing in church, but it's a lot more than that, too.   It's about enjoying the wonderful world God has made.   It's about how we speak to each other.   It's about how we live our lives.

As you pray you can:

thank God for his goodness and his help;

tell God how great he is, and that you love him;

ask God to help you, your friends, your family and other people.

If you are a helper using this book with someone who does not read, you will find guidance notes at the end.

The *Easy-to-Read Version* of the Bible is available to buy from Causeway PROSPECTS.

Songs of praise

The heavens speak about God's glory. The skies tell about the good things his hands have made.
Psalm 19:1 (Full reading Psalm 19:1,2)

A psalm is a song of praise to God. King David loved God and wrote many of the psalms. He wrote the two psalms we will be looking at in this book, Psalms 19 and 20. These psalms both tell us a bit about God and a bit about King David.

In the psalms we find things to thank God for. We find out things about God that will make us full of joy. We will find out how to live well. And we will want to praise God because he is so good.

Dear God, thank you for King David and for these songs of praise. Please send your Holy Spirit to help me to praise you each day. Amen.

God made everything

The heavens speak about God's glory. The skies tell about the good things his hands have made.
Psalm 19:1 (Full reading Psalm 19:1,2)

The first chapter in the Bible (Genesis chapter 1) tells us how God made everything. This psalm tells us about some of the things God made.

God made the sun and the sky. He made all the people that live on the earth. God made the day and the night. Each time we see the sky we can remember that God made it. Each morning when we wake we can remember that God made the day and the night.

And when we remember we can say 'Thank you' to God.

Thank you God for rest at night. Thank you for a place to sleep. Thank you for each new morning. Thank you, Father God. Amen.

3 Learn from the sky

The heavens speak about God's glory. The skies tell about the good things his hands have made.
Psalm 19:1 (Full reading Psalm 19:1,2)

Have you ever watched a really beautiful sunset or sunrise? Maybe the light of the sun was making the clouds look different colours. Sometimes clouds look pink. Sometimes they look orange, sometimes red. Sometimes there are just a few clouds, sometimes lots of them.

This verse tells us that looking at the sky can help us to understand God. Seeing a beautiful sunrise can teach us about God. He loves to make beautiful shapes and colours. He wants us to see them and enjoy them. And as we look we can remember – God made that. And thank him.

Thank you God for the colours in a beautiful sunrise or sunset. Thank you for every lovely thing you have made. Help me to enjoy them more and more. Amen.

Each new day tells more of the story. And each night reveals more and more about God's power. Psalm 19:2 (Full reading Psalm 19:1,2)

Wouldn't it be boring if every day was the same? If you live near a river or the sea you will know that it looks different every day. Sometimes the wind makes ripples on the water. Even the waves are all different from each other. There might be birds or even fish to see. Sometimes the trees bend over in the wind.

You cannot count the different things God has made and done – there are so many things. He is a God who loves to make lots of different things. This is something you can easily remember every day. Just look outside!

Dear God, when I am out with my friends and we see beautiful things, help me to talk about how you have made them for us to enjoy. Amen.

5 So many stars

Each new day tells more of the story. And each night reveals more and more about God's power. Psalm 19:2 (Full reading Psalm 19:1,2)

Some nights when you look up into the sky you can see just a few stars. If it is a really clear night and there aren't any street lights you might be able to see lots of stars. You could try to count them but it's very hard because there are so many. There are more stars than anyone can count!

God made every one of the stars and put them in their places in the sky. This tells us about how strong and powerful God is. He is more powerful than any king or army on earth.

Dear God, help me to remember that you are a powerful God. You can do anything. I praise you. Amen.

6 God knows all about you

Each new day tells more of the story. And each night reveals more and more about God's power.
Psalm 19:2 (Full reading Psalm 19:1,2)

During the day you can't see the stars, can you? But they are still there. And during the night you can't see the sun. But the sun is still in the place where God put it. It's just that you don't see the light of the sun when it's night time.

You can't see God. But you know where he is. God is in heaven. God knows all about you and he hears your prayers. When you need help, ask Father God and he will send the Holy Spirit to help you.

Father God, please send your Holy Spirit to help me. Amen.

7 Look around you

Each new day tells more of the story. And each night reveals more and more about God's power. You can't really hear any speech or words. They don't make any sound we can hear.
Psalm 19:2,3 (Full reading Psalm 19:2–4)

So far we have been thinking about some of the wonderful things God has made. He made the sea and sky, the rivers and trees, birds, flowers and mountains. So many different things, so many lovely shapes and colours. People call it the beauty of nature. And God made it.

God made the world for us to enjoy. But God also made the world so that people will know that there is a God. God made all these things so that people can find out about him. All they have to do is look at the world around them.

Think about your friend (say their name) who is not sure about God.

Dear God, please help my friend to believe in you because of the wonderful things they see around them. Amen.

Each new day tells more of the story. And each night reveals more and more about God's power ... their 'voice' goes throughout the world. Their 'words' go to the ends of the earth.
Psalm 19:2,4 (Full reading Psalm 19:2–4)

One day when you are outside try closing your eyes. What can you hear? If you are in a town you might hear cars or people shouting. If you are in the country you might hear birds singing or a waterfall. You might hear the wind in the trees.

These sounds help us to think about God, too. When you hear a bird sing or a dog bark remember that God made birds and dogs. When you hear the wind in the trees remember that God made the wind and he made the trees.

In your prayers today remember some of the sounds that make you think of God. Then thank God for them.

**But their 'voice' goes throughout the world.
Their 'words' go to the ends of the earth.**
Psalm 19:4 (Full reading Psalm 19:1–4)

Holidays are good times to enjoy the things that God has made. Usually when we are on holiday we have more time to look at the things around us. Often we are with someone and we can enjoy doing things together. Often our holiday is in a nice place. There is lots to see and we can be outside more. Perhaps the sun shines for us.

Think about a holiday you had. Perhaps you can look at a photo from the holiday. Thank God for the holiday and for the people who helped you to have a good time.

Read out loud the first four verses of Psalm 19 or ask someone to read them for you. Then thank God for all the good things he makes for us to enjoy. Thank him for good times like holidays.

10   A job to do

The sky is like a home for the sun. The sun comes out like a happy bridegroom from his bedroom. The sun begins its path across the sky like an athlete eager to run his race.
Psalm 19:4,5 (Full reading Psalm 19:4–6)

Have you ever seen photos from a wedding? The people are always smiling! The bridegroom and his bride are happy because they are now husband and wife.

God put the sun in the sky and gave it a job to do. The sun's job is to give us daylight. And God gives each one of us a job to do. Maybe you already know what that is. There may be more than one job God wants you to do.

In your prayers today ask God to show you what he wants you to do. Then ask him to help you to do what he wants. These are big prayers to pray. You might not get an answer straightaway, but keep asking. God will show you the things he wants you to do.

11 What can you do?

The sky is like a home for the sun. The sun comes out like a happy bridegroom from his bedroom. The sun begins its path across the sky like an athlete eager to run his race.
Psalm 19:4,5 (Full reading Psalm 19:4–6)

So what is it that God wants you to do? There are some things that every Christian should do. Things like finding out what the Bible says and what it means for us. And trying to live in a way that pleases God.

But then there are things that are different for each person. God wants some people to be teachers but not everybody. God wants some people to take care of children but not everybody. There are some things that everybody can do. Like giving a smile to cheer somebody up.

Pray for one of your friends or someone in your family. Ask God what you could do to help them or to make them feel better.

The Lord's teachings are perfect. They give strength to God's people. The Lord's Agreement [set of commands] can be trusted. It helps foolish people become wise. The Lord's laws are right. They make people happy. The Lord's commands are good. They show people the right way to live.
Psalm 19:7,8 (Full reading Psalm 19:7–10)

We know that God is perfect. He is always right. He never does anything wrong. He always knows the right things to say and do. If a person knows the right things to say and do, others will say that he or she is wise. What about you? Would you like to be wise? This verse tells us how.

The Bible says 'the Lord's teachings' help to make us wise. So keep reading or listening to the Bible and finding out what it means.

Father God, thank you that the Bible will help to make me wise. Please send Christian friends to help me understand more of what the Bible says. Amen.

13 Learning how to live

The Lord's teachings are perfect. They give strength to God's people. The Lord's Agreement [set of commands] can be trusted. It helps foolish people become wise. The Lord's laws are right. They make people happy. The Lord's commands are good. They show people the right way to live.
Psalm 19:7,8 (Full reading Psalm 19:7–10)

These verses tell us that the Bible ('the Lord's teachings') makes us strong and wise and happy. It tells us something else too; the Bible tells us how to live.

If you love Jesus you will want to live in a good way. If you love Jesus you will want to do things that please Father God in heaven, things that help other people around you.

Dear God, please send your Holy Spirit to help me do the things that always please you. Amen.

14 Worship is like a light

The Lord's laws are right. They make people happy. The Lord's commands are good. They show people the right way to live. Worshipping the Lord is like a light that will shine bright forever. The Lord's judgements are good and fair. They are completely right.
Psalm 19:8,9 (Full reading Psalm 19:8–11)

Not long ago I went into a hut used for watching birds. When we went in it was very dark. We couldn't see each other. We couldn't see any birds. Then we opened some wooden coverings over the windows (called shutters). When we did that we could see inside to walk about. And we could see outside as well. We could enjoy the beauty of the lake and watch the birds.

Worshipping God is like opening those windows. God shows us new things when we worship. Worshipping God is telling him he is great and that you love him.

In your prayers today tell God how much you love him or use this prayer: Dear God, I think you're great, I love you. Amen.

15 God's good teaching

Worshipping the Lord is like a light that will shine bright forever. The Lord's judgements are good and fair. They are completely right. The Lord's teachings are worth more than the best gold. They are sweeter than the best honey that comes straight from the honeycomb.
Psalm 19:9,10 (Full reading Psalm 19:9–11)

Do you remember that King David wrote this psalm? King David wanted us to know that the things God teaches us are very important. They are good for us. King David said that having God's teaching is better than having gold.

If we have God's teaching we will feel even better than after we've eaten something really nice like honey. God's teaching really is good for us.

Dear God, help me to learn from your teaching so I can live like you want me to. Amen.

The Lord's teachings warn his servant. Good things come from obeying them. No person can see all of his own mistakes. So don't let me do secret sins.
Psalm 19:11,12 (Full reading Psalm 19:11–14)

Do you sometimes make mistakes? Everyone does! It's really hard to get things right all the time, isn't it! Sometimes you can tell straightaway if you've done something wrong. Then you can put it right. You can say sorry if you've upset someone or clear up if you've made a mess.

Sometimes you don't know if you've done something wrong. Sometimes you cannot tell. Perhaps someone else has to tell you. Today's verses tell us that reading the Bible helps us to know what is right and what is wrong, what is good and what is bad.

In your prayers, ask God to show you anything you have done or are thinking of doing that is wrong. Ask God to show you the things he doesn't like. Then say 'Lord, I am sorry'.

17 Saying sorry to God

The Lord's teachings warn his servant. Good things come from obeying them. No person can see all his own mistakes. So don't let me do secret sins ... If you help me, then I can be pure and free from my sins. I hope my words and thoughts please you.
Psalm 19:11–14 (Full reading Psalm 19:11–14)

When we read the Bible and talk with other Christians we find out what is right and good. God is pleased when we do those things.

Sometimes we do something wrong even though we know it's wrong. We should not do it but we do. Do you find you sometimes do that? It makes God sad so we must say sorry to him. But how do we stop doing those bad things? How do we do good things instead? We need God's help.

Let's use the words of verse 13 of this psalm as our prayer today: Lord, don't let me do the sins I want to do. Don't let those sins rule me. If you help me then I can be pure and free from my sins. Amen.

18 Set free from sin

Don't let me do the sins I want to do. Don't let those sins rule me. If you help me, then I can be pure and free from my sins. I hope my words and thoughts please you. Lord, you are my Rock – you are the One who saves me.
Psalm 19:13,14 (Full reading Psalm 19:12–14)

Jesus is the one who came to save us and set us free from our sins. When Jesus died on the cross he made it possible for us to be forgiven.

First, you must believe that Jesus died for you. Then you must say sorry to God for anything you have done or said that hurt another person or made God sad. And God will forgive you.

When God forgives you for something, he will never remember that thing again. He will not punish you for it – Jesus took the punishment on the cross. That's what it means to be set free from our sins.

Thank you, Jesus, for dying on the cross so that I can be forgiven. Amen.

 # Thank God for Jesus

Don't let me do the sins I want to do. Don't let those sins rule me. If you help me, then I can be pure and free from my sins. I hope my words and thoughts please you. Lord, you are my Rock – you are the One who saves me.
Psalm 19:13,14 (Full reading Psalm 19:12–14)

We should thank Father God every day for Jesus, and for everything Jesus has done for us. God is pleased when we say thank you.

God will help us to please him. God will send us his Holy Spirit. The Holy Spirit works in everyone who loves Jesus. The Holy Spirit helps those people to say things and think things that please God – things like worshipping God, praying for our friends and thinking about God's teachings. These are all things that please God. We call God our Rock because he is strong and we can trust him.

In your prayers today think about some good things God has done and thank him for them. Then ask him to send the Holy Spirit to help you and any of your friends who need help.

May the Lord answer your call for help when you have troubles.
Psalm 20:1 (Full reading Psalm 20:1–3)

Prayer is talking and listening to God.

What do you do when you talk to a friend? You tell the friend about yourself so they find out how you're feeling and what you've been doing. You listen to what your friend says so you find out about them. You find out what they like and what they are thinking. You can laugh together. You can ask for help.

God wants you to talk to him just like you talk to a friend. And he wants you to listen to him too.

Dear God, help me to talk to you like I talk to a friend. Help me to get used to listening to you as well. Amen.

21 The Holy Spirit

May God send you help from his Holy Place. May he support you from Zion [God's holy mountain].

Psalm 20:2 (Full reading Psalm 20:1–3)

When you pray, God sends help in different ways. Today we will think about how the Holy Spirit helps.

Who is the Holy Spirit? The Holy Spirit is God at work on the earth.

The Holy Spirit can help you. Perhaps you are worried about something so you pray for yourself. God will send his Holy Spirit to you to give you peace. After that you will not need to worry any more.

The Holy Spirit can help the people you pray for. Perhaps a friend is ill. When you pray, God will send his Holy Spirit to make your friend better or take away the pain.

Have you any friends who are ill? Say their names and ask God to send his Holy Spirit to help them.

22 God sends a person

May God send you help from his Holy Place. May he support you from Zion [God's holy mountain].
Psalm 20:2 (Full reading Psalm 20:1–3)

Today we think about how God answers a prayer by sending a person. Let's say someone called Jane is feeling sad or fed up. Perhaps she has had a bad day or even a bad week. What she needs is someone to cheer her up.

When you pray for Jane, this is what can happen. The Holy Spirit speaks to one of Jane's friends. Let's call her Susan. Susan thinks, 'I think I'll call on Jane'. Then Susan goes to see Jane and cheers her up.

That's how it works. God sends people to answer prayers. Susan's visit to Jane is an answer to prayer.

Lord, thank you for answering prayer by sending people. Help me to keep praying for people who need God's help. Amen.

23 God uses your gifts

**May God remember all the gifts you offered.
May he accept all your sacrifices [gifts to God].**
Psalm 20:3 (Full reading Psalm 20:1–3)

Have you ever thought that you could be an answer to prayer? With God's help you can!

Everyone who loves the Lord Jesus has a special gift from God. That gift is being able to do something that will bless or help other people.

As you pray for someone, God might ask you to use one of your special gifts for that person. Maybe you're good at talking with people and cheering them up. Maybe you're good at remembering people's birthdays and sending them a card.

Ask God to help you use the things you can do to make other people feel better.

Dear God, thank you for the things I can do that bless other people. Please show me who needs a bit of help or who needs to hear from me. Amen.

24 'Happy to give' people

May God remember all the gifts you offered.
May he accept all of your sacrifices.
Psalm 20:3 (Full reading Psalm 20:1–3)

A sacrifice is sometimes doing without something because you give that thing to someone else. Some people call this 'putting other people first'. It means that you have a bit less because you've given some away.

Making a sacrifice might mean giving some of your money or things you have to help someone else. It could also mean giving some of your time to help others.

Thinking more about other people than about yourself is an important part of Jesus' teaching. When you put other people first in your prayers or use your time or your money for others, you are doing what God wants you to do. God wants us to be generous, 'happy to give' people.

Dear God, please show me who needs my prayers and my help. Please make me into a 'happy to give' person. Amen.

25 What you really want

May God remember all the gifts you offered. May he accept all your sacrifices. May God give you what you really want. May he make all your plans successful.
Psalm 20:3,4 (Full reading Psalm 20:1–4)

Most people have hopes and dreams – things they long for, things they really want.

Maybe you're waiting to meet someone who will be a really good close friend. Maybe you'd like to move to a nicer place to live. Maybe you'd really like to understand the Bible better. Maybe you've started to play the piano or to read and you'd like to be really good at it. Whatever it is that you really want, God knows about it.

As well as praying and giving to others we can pray for ourselves and our hopes and dreams. God is a 'happy to give' person and he wants to give good things to us.

In your prayers today talk to God about the things you really want for yourself. Then day by day watch out for the answers to your prayers.

26 Help with your plans

May God give you what you really want. May he make all your plans successful.
Psalm 20:4 (Full reading Psalm 20:4,5)

When someone wants to build a new house they have to think and plan ahead. What will it look like? Who will build it? How many bricks and how much cement is needed?

Do you remember your last holiday? Holidays take a lot of planning. You have to work out where you want to go and when. You have to find somewhere to stay, and plan how to get there. For a day at the seaside you will need to plan what food and beach games to take.

But plans don't always work out do they? Something might go wrong that changes everything. The car could break down on the way to the seaside. If someone gets ill before the holiday you might not be able to go.

Father God, please watch over my plans and my friends' plans and make them happen. Amen.

27 Show that you care

We will be happy when God helps you. Let's praise God's name. May the Lord give you everything that you ask for!
Psalm 20:5 (Full reading Psalm 20:4,5)

Imagine you have some friends who have problems and need God's help. They are Christians and you have been praying for them. Then you meet your friends and say to them, 'I will be happy when God helps you'.

Saying this will help them believe that God is going to answer your prayers. And it shows that you really care about your friends. And when God answers your prayers for them you will be happy and give thanks to God.

Think of someone you've been praying for who needs God's help. Try to say or send the words of today's verse to them. Say or write your friend's name first: ' ... I will be happy when God helps you. Let's praise God's name. I hope the Lord gives you everything you ask for.' Amen.

28 God is powerful

**Now, I know the Lord helps the king he chose!
God was in his holy heaven, and he answered
his chosen king. God used his great power to
save the king.**
Psalm 20:6 (Full reading Psalm 20:6,7)

Have you ever been at the seaside when the sea
was rough and the waves were breaking onto
the rocks? The sea is very powerful.

If you stand by a big waterfall the sound is
very loud like a roar. Water is powerful when
it is like that. In some places people use falling
water to make electricity so we can have light
and heat in our homes.

God is powerful. God is more powerful than the
biggest wave or waterfall. God used his power
to help King David. God will use his power to
help the people we pray for.

**Dear God, thank you that you are a powerful
God. Please show your power today by
helping the people I care about and pray for.
Amen.**

29 Trust in God

Some people trust their chariots. Other people trust their soldiers. But we remember the Lord our God.

Psalm 20:7 (Full reading Psalm 20:6–8)

When King David wrote this psalm he was remembering a battle. His enemies had horses and special carts for the horses to pull called chariots and lots of soldiers riding in the chariots. King David's enemies said, 'Because we have strong things like chariots and soldiers we will win the battle'.

King David did not have these strong things. He asked God to help him and he believed that God would help.

We may not have many things or people to help us. But God is powerful. We can put our trust in him. Trusting God is more important than having many things.

Dear God, help me to believe that you will hear my prayer. Show your power where it is needed. Help me to trust you more each day. Amen.

30 Be thankful

Some people trust their chariots. Other people trust their soldiers. But we remember the Lord our God. Those other people were defeated – they died in battle. But we won! We are the winners!
Psalm 20:7,8 (Full reading Psalm 20:7–9)

King David trusted in God. God helped the king and his men in the battle so that they were the winners. God answered their prayers. King David was happy as he thought about the good things God had done.

You have prayed lots of prayers while reading this book. Think about some of the things and people you have prayed for. Try to remember some of the things God has done. How has God answered your prayers? How did God show his power?

**In your prayers today, thank God for everything he has done. You could finish with this prayer: God of power and love, I worship you. Thank you for hearing my prayers.
Thank you for all the answers to my prayers.
Amen.**

Key words

Amen — We usually say this at the end of prayers and it means, 'That's my prayer too'.

Bless — To show kindness to someone. To do them a good turn.

Cross — To be cross is to be angry, bad-tempered.

Cross — A cross is two big pieces of wood in the shape of a cross. Jesus was nailed to a cross when he was killed.

Foolish — Silly.

Forgive — When you forgive someone who has hurt you, you're not cross with them anymore.

Holy Spirit — The Holy Spirit is a person. He is the third person of the Trinity with Father God and Jesus, his Son. The Holy Spirit is God at work on the earth.

Judgement — Deciding what is right and what is wrong.

Lord — The one in charge. Another word for God.

Peace — Quiet, calm, not worrying.

Powerful — Strong.

Praise	To tell God (or a person) how good they are.
Pray	Talk to God or Jesus about things.
Psalm	A song written to God.
Punishment	What happens to a person who is caught doing something bad or wrong.
Rule	To rule is to be in charge.
Save	To rescue, set free, or keep safe.
Sin / Sins	Bad things people do that make God sad and hurt other people.
Worship	Telling God how much you love him through words or songs or things you do.

Notes for carers and helpers

These Bible notes are designed to help a wide a range of people who need extra help. It's impossible to tailor Bible notes to fit everyone's needs. But our hope is that many who have some level of visual or intellectual disability or just need a simpler approach can be helped to pray and read the Bible regularly through this series.

Some people will be able to use these notes without any help from others. But if you are the carer or helper of someone needing some assistance with using them, here are a few pointers which may be useful to you.

Before you begin, ask the Holy Spirit to help communicate the main thought from each reading and note to the person you are reading with. God through the Holy Spirit can communicate on levels that we cannot! Part of the Holy Spirit's role is to make Jesus real to people and you are working in partnership with him.

Make sure you have the person's full attention before starting to read. Think about how you can eliminate auditory or visual distractions in the environment such as TV or other people. Try to find a quiet place. Use eye contact to maintain good connection.

Read slowly and clearly, pausing where suitable. Facial expressions, hand and body movements can all help to underline the meaning of the material. Encourage whatever response is appropriate, particularly in prayer and praise.

Use your knowledge of the person to assess how much is being understood, how much clarification might be needed and how to best make applications more relevant.

Make your time together an opportunity for learning and fellowship for both of you.

Other titles in the
Bible Prospects series:

Being like Jesus

The story of Christmas

God gives new life

Scripture Union produces a wide range of Bible reading notes for people of all ages, and Bible-based material for small groups. SU publications are available from any Christian bookshop. For information and to request free samples and a free catalogue of Bible resources:

- phone SU's mail order line: local rate number 08450 706 006

- email info@scriptureunion.org.uk

- fax 01908 856020

- log on to www.scriptureunion.org.uk

- write to SU Mail Order, PO Box 5148,